PERSONAL INFORMATION

Name	
Address	
Mobile	Work
Email	Fax

COMPANY INFORMATION

Company	
Address	
Phone	Email
Fax	Website

EMERGENCY CONTACT

Name	Name
Phone	Phone
Doctor's Name	Preferred Hospital
Phone	Phone
Police	Paramedic
Fire	Poison Control Center

JOB INFO			
Project/Job		Date	
Contract #		Day	
Location		Weather	
Foreman		AM	PM
Was work delayed for any reason?		☐ Yes ☐ No Describe in Notes	

EMPLOYEES	Employee/General	Hrs	Work Performed

SUBCONTRACTORS	Subcontractor	Men	Hrs	Work Performed

NOTES

ADDITIONAL INFO		
Inspections	
Visitors	
Material Delivery	
Equipment on Site	
Rental Tools	

SAFETY

☐ No Injuries

☐ Are project wide power cords in good working condition?

☐ Is project wide fall protection in place?

☐ Are there ladders on the project?

☐ If yes, have any ladders been modified?

☐ Are there any lifts on the project?

☐ Is the lift's certificate current?

☐ Are all workers wearing proper PPE?

☐ Is confined space entry required?

☐ If yes, are all safety measures being followed?

JOB INFO		
Project/Job	Date	
Contract #	Day	
Location	Weather	
Foreman	AM	PM
Was work delayed for any reason?	☐ Yes ☐ No	Describe in Notes

EMPLOYEES

Employee/General	Hrs	Work Performed

SUBCONTRACTORS

Subcontractor	Men	Hrs	Work Performed

NOTES

ADDITIONAL INFO

Inspections	
Visitors	
Material Delivery	
Equipment on Site	
Rental Tools	

SAFETY

☐ No Injuries

☐ Are project wide power cords in good working condition?

☐ Is project wide fall protection in place?

☐ Are there ladders on the project?

☐ If yes, have any ladders been modified?

☐ Are there any lifts on the project?

☐ Is the lift's certificate current?

☐ Are all workers wearing proper PPE?

☐ Is confined space entry required?

☐ If yes, are all safety measures being followed?

JOB INFO				
Project/Job		Date		
Contract #		Day		
Location		Weather		
Foreman		AM		PM
Was work delayed for any reason?		☐ Yes ☐ No	Describe in Notes	

EMPLOYEES

Employee/General	Hrs	Work Performed

SUBCONTRACTORS

Subcontractor	Men	Hrs	Work Performed

NOTES

ADDITIONAL INFO

Inspections	
Visitors	
Material Delivery	
Equipment on Site	
Rental Tools	

SAFETY

☐ No Injuries

☐ Are project wide power cords in good working condition?

☐ Is project wide fall protection in place?

☐ Are there ladders on the project?

☐ If yes, have any ladders been modified?

☐ Are there any lifts on the project?

☐ Is the lift's certificate current?

☐ Are all workers wearing proper PPE?

☐ Is confined space entry required?

☐ If yes, are all safety measures being followed?

JOB INFO			
Project/Job		Date	
Contract #		Day	
Location		Weather	
Foreman		AM	PM
Was work delayed for any reason?		☐ Yes ☐ No	Describe in Notes

EMPLOYEES

Employee/General	Hrs	Work Performed

SUBCONTRACTORS

Subcontractor	Men	Hrs	Work Performed

NOTES

ADDITIONAL INFO

Inspections	
Visitors	
Material Delivery	
Equipment on Site	
Rental Tools	

SAFETY

☐ No Injuries

☐ Are project wide power cords in good working condition?

☐ Is project wide fall protection in place?

☐ Are there ladders on the project?

☐ If yes, have any ladders been modified?

☐ Are there any lifts on the project?

☐ Is the lift's certificate current?

☐ Are all workers wearing proper PPE?

☐ Is confined space entry required?

☐ If yes, are all safety measures being followed?

JOB INFO		
Project/Job	Date	
Contract #	Day	
Location	Weather	
Foreman	AM	PM
Was work delayed for any reason?	☐ Yes ☐ No	Describe in Notes

EMPLOYEES

Employee/General	Hrs	Work Performed

SUBCONTRACTORS

Subcontractor	Men	Hrs	Work Performed

NOTES

ADDITIONAL INFO

Inspections	
Visitors	
Material Delivery	
Equipment on Site	
Rental Tools	

SAFETY

☐ No Injuries
☐ Are project wide power cords in good working condition?
☐ Is project wide fall protection in place?
☐ Are there ladders on the project?
☐ If yes, have any ladders been modified?

☐ Are there any lifts on the project?
☐ Is the lift's certificate current?
☐ Are all workers wearing proper PPE?
☐ Is confined space entry required?
☐ If yes, are all safety measures being followed?

JOB INFO			
Project/Job		Date	
Contract #		Day	
Location		Weather	
Foreman		AM	PM
Was work delayed for any reason?		☐ Yes ☐ No Describe in Notes	

EMPLOYEES

Employee/General	Hrs	Work Performed

SUBCONTRACTORS

Subcontractor	Men	Hrs	Work Performed

NOTES

ADDITIONAL INFO

Inspections	
Visitors	
Material Delivery	
Equipment on Site	
Rental Tools	

SAFETY

☐ No Injuries

☐ Are project wide power cords in good working condition?

☐ Is project wide fall protection in place?

☐ Are there ladders on the project?

☐ If yes, have any ladders been modified?

☐ Are there any lifts on the project?

☐ Is the lift's certificate current?

☐ Are all workers wearing proper PPE?

☐ Is confined space entry required?

☐ If yes, are all safety measures being followed?

JOB INFO		
Project/Job	Date	
Contract #	Day	
Location	Weather	
Foreman	AM	PM
Was work delayed for any reason?	☐Yes ☐ No	Describe in Notes

EMPLOYEES

Employee/General	Hrs	Work Performed

SUBCONTRACTORS

Subcontractor	Men	Hrs	Work Performed

NOTES

ADDITIONAL INFO

Inspections	
Visitors	
Material Delivery	
Equipment on Site	
Rental Tools	

SAFETY

☐ No Injuries

☐ Are project wide power cords in good working condition?

☐ Is project wide fall protection in place?

☐ Are there ladders on the project?

☐ If yes, have any ladders been modified?

☐ Are there any lifts on the project?

☐ Is the lift's certificate current?

☐ Are all workers wearing proper PPE?

☐ Is confined space entry required?

☐ If yes, are all safety measures being followed?

JOB INFO					
Project/Job			Date		
Contract #			Day		
Location			Weather		
Foreman			AM	PM	
Was work delayed for any reason?			☐Yes ☐No	Describe in Notes	

EMPLOYEES		
Employee/General	Hrs	Work Performed

SUBCONTRACTORS			
Subcontractor	Men	Hrs	Work Performed

NOTES

ADDITIONAL INFO	
Inspections	
Visitors	
Material Delivery	
Equipment on Site	
Rental Tools	

SAFETY

☐ No Injuries
☐ Are project wide power cords in good working condition?
☐ Is project wide fall protection in place?
☐ Are there ladders on the project?
☐ If yes, have any ladders been modified?

☐ Are there any lifts on the project?
☐ Is the lift's certificate current?
☐ Are all workers wearing proper PPE?
☐ Is confined space entry required?
☐ If yes, are all safety measures being followed?

JOB INFO			
Project/Job		Date	
Contract #		Day	
Location		Weather	
Foreman		AM	PM
Was work delayed for any reason?		☐Yes ☐ No	Describe in Notes

EMPLOYEES		
Employee/General	Hrs	Work Performed

SUBCONTRACTORS			
Subcontractor	Men	Hrs	Work Performed

NOTES

ADDITIONAL INFO	
Inspections	
Visitors	
Material Delivery	
Equipment on Site	
Rental Tools	

SAFETY

☐ No Injuries
☐ Are project wide power cords in good working condition?
☐ Is project wide fall protection in place?
☐ Are there ladders on the project?
☐ If yes, have any ladders been modified?

☐ Are there any lifts on the project?
☐ Is the lift's certificate current?
☐ Are all workers wearing proper PPE?
☐ Is confined space entry required?
☐ If yes, are all safety measures being followed?

JOB INFO			
Project/Job		Date	
Contract #		Day	
Location		Weather	
Foreman		AM	PM
Was work delayed for any reason?		☐ Yes ☐ No	Describe in Notes

EMPLOYEES

Employee/General	Hrs	Work Performed

SUBCONTRACTORS

Subcontractor	Men	Hrs	Work Performed

NOTES

ADDITIONAL INFO

Inspections	
Visitors	
Material Delivery	
Equipment on Site	
Rental Tools	

SAFETY

☐ No Injuries

☐ Are project wide power cords in good working condition?

☐ Is project wide fall protection in place?

☐ Are there ladders on the project?

☐ If yes, have any ladders been modified?

☐ Are there any lifts on the project?

☐ Is the lift's certificate current?

☐ Are all workers wearing proper PPE?

☐ Is confined space entry required?

☐ If yes, are all safety measures being followed?

JOB INFO				
Project/Job		Date		
Contract #		Day		
Location		Weather		
Foreman		AM		PM
Was work delayed for any reason?		☐ Yes ☐ No Describe in Notes		

EMPLOYEES

Employee/General	Hrs	Work Performed

SUBCONTRACTORS

Subcontractor	Men	Hrs	Work Performed

NOTES

ADDITIONAL INFO

Inspections	
Visitors	
Material Delivery	
Equipment on Site	
Rental Tools	

SAFETY

- ☐ No Injuries
- ☐ Are project wide power cords in good working condition?
- ☐ Is project wide fall protection in place?
- ☐ Are there ladders on the project?
- ☐ If yes, have any ladders been modified?
- ☐ Are there any lifts on the project?
- ☐ Is the lift's certificate current?
- ☐ Are all workers wearing proper PPE?
- ☐ Is confined space entry required?
- ☐ If yes, are all safety measures being followed?

JOB INFO		
Project/Job	Date	
Contract #	Day	
Location	Weather	
Foreman	AM	PM
Was work delayed for any reason?	☐ Yes ☐ No	Describe in Notes

EMPLOYEES

Employee/General	Hrs	Work Performed

SUBCONTRACTORS

Subcontractor	Men	Hrs	Work Performed

NOTES

ADDITIONAL INFO

Inspections	
Visitors	
Material Delivery	
Equipment on Site	
Rental Tools	

SAFETY

☐ No Injuries
☐ Are project wide power cords in good working condition?
☐ Is project wide fall protection in place?
☐ Are there ladders on the project?
☐ If yes, have any ladders been modified?

☐ Are there any lifts on the project?
☐ Is the lift's certificate current?
☐ Are all workers wearing proper PPE?
☐ Is confined space entry required?
☐ If yes, are all safety measures being followed?

JOB INFO		
Project/Job	Date	
Contract #	Day	
Location	Weather	
Foreman	AM	PM
Was work delayed for any reason?	☐ Yes ☐ No	Describe in Notes

EMPLOYEES

Employee/General	Hrs	Work Performed

SUBCONTRACTORS

Subcontractor	Men	Hrs	Work Performed

NOTES

ADDITIONAL INFO

Inspections	
Visitors	
Material Delivery	
Equipment on Site	
Rental Tools	

SAFETY

☐ No Injuries   ☐ Are there any lifts on the project?
☐ Are project wide power cords in good working condition?   ☐ Is the lift's certificate current?
☐ Is project wide fall protection in place?   ☐ Are all workers wearing proper PPE?
☐ Are there ladders on the project?   ☐ Is confined space entry required?
☐ If yes, have any ladders been modified?   ☐ If yes, are all safety measures being followed?

JOB INFO			
Project/Job		Date	
Contract #		Day	
Location		Weather	
Foreman		AM	PM
Was work delayed for any reason?		☐Yes ☐No Describe in Notes	

EMPLOYEES

Employee/General	Hrs	Work Performed

SUBCONTRACTORS

Subcontractor	Men	Hrs	Work Performed

NOTES

ADDITIONAL INFO

Inspections	
Visitors	
Material Delivery	
Equipment on Site	
Rental Tools	

SAFETY

☐ No Injuries
☐ Are project wide power cords in good working condition?
☐ Is project wide fall protection in place?
☐ Are there ladders on the project?
☐ If yes, have any ladders been modified?

☐ Are there any lifts on the project?
☐ Is the lift's certificate current?
☐ Are all workers wearing proper PPE?
☐ Is confined space entry required?
☐ If yes, are all safety measures being followed?

JOB INFO		
Project/Job	Date	
Contract #	Day	
Location	Weather	
Foreman	AM	PM
Was work delayed for any reason?	☐Yes ☐ No	Describe in Notes

EMPLOYEES

Employee/General	Hrs	Work Performed

SUBCONTRACTORS

Subcontractor	Men	Hrs	Work Performed

NOTES

ADDITIONAL INFO

Inspections	
Visitors	
Material Delivery	
Equipment on Site	
Rental Tools	

SAFETY

☐ No Injuries
☐ Are project wide power cords in good working condition?
☐ Is project wide fall protection in place?
☐ Are there ladders on the project?
☐ If yes, have any ladders been modified?

☐ Are there any lifts on the project?
☐ Is the lift's certificate current?
☐ Are all workers wearing proper PPE?
☐ Is confined space entry required?
☐ If yes, are all safety measures being followed?

JOB INFO			
Project/Job		Date	
Contract #		Day	
Location		Weather	
Foreman		AM	PM
Was work delayed for any reason?		☐ Yes ☐ No Describe in Notes	

EMPLOYEES

Employee/General	Hrs	Work Performed

SUBCONTRACTORS

Subcontractor	Men	Hrs	Work Performed

NOTES

ADDITIONAL INFO

Inspections	
Visitors	
Material Delivery	
Equipment on Site	
Rental Tools	

SAFETY

☐ No Injuries

☐ Are project wide power cords in good working condition?

☐ Is project wide fall protection in place?

☐ Are there ladders on the project?

☐ If yes, have any ladders been modified?

☐ Are there any lifts on the project?

☐ Is the lift's certificate current?

☐ Are all workers wearing proper PPE?

☐ Is confined space entry required?

☐ If yes, are all safety measures being followed?

JOB INFO				
Project/Job		Date		
Contract #		Day		
Location		Weather		
Foreman		AM		PM
Was work delayed for any reason?		☐ Yes	☐ No	Describe in Notes

EMPLOYEES

Employee/General	Hrs	Work Performed

SUBCONTRACTORS

Subcontractor	Men	Hrs	Work Performed

NOTES

ADDITIONAL INFO

Inspections	
Visitors	
Material Delivery	
Equipment on Site	
Rental Tools	

SAFETY

☐ No Injuries	☐ Are there any lifts on the project?
☐ Are project wide power cords in good working condition?	☐ Is the lift's certificate current?
☐ Is project wide fall protection in place?	☐ Are all workers wearing proper PPE?
☐ Are there ladders on the project?	☐ Is confined space entry required?
☐ If yes, have any ladders been modified?	☐ If yes, are all safety measures being followed?

JOB INFO

Project/Job	Date
Contract #	Day
Location	Weather
Foreman	AM PM
Was work delayed for any reason?	☐ Yes ☐ No Describe in Notes

EMPLOYEES

Employee/General	Hrs	Work Performed

SUBCONTRACTORS

Subcontractor	Men	Hrs	Work Performed

NOTES

ADDITIONAL INFO

Inspections	
Visitors	
Material Delivery	
Equipment on Site	
Rental Tools	

SAFETY

☐ No Injuries

☐ Are project wide power cords in good working condition?

☐ Is project wide fall protection in place?

☐ Are there ladders on the project?

☐ If yes, have any ladders been modified?

☐ Are there any lifts on the project?

☐ Is the lift's certificate current?

☐ Are all workers wearing proper PPE?

☐ Is confined space entry required?

☐ If yes, are all safety measures being followed?

JOB INFO		
Project/Job	Date	
Contract #	Day	
Location	Weather	
Foreman	AM	PM
Was work delayed for any reason?	☐ Yes ☐ No Describe in Notes	

EMPLOYEES

Employee/General	Hrs	Work Performed

SUBCONTRACTORS

Subcontractor	Men	Hrs	Work Performed

NOTES

ADDITIONAL INFO

Inspections	
Visitors	
Material Delivery	
Equipment on Site	
Rental Tools	

SAFETY

☐ No Injuries

☐ Are project wide power cords in good working condition?

☐ Is project wide fall protection in place?

☐ Are there ladders on the project?

☐ If yes, have any ladders been modified?

☐ Are there any lifts on the project?

☐ Is the lift's certificate current?

☐ Are all workers wearing proper PPE?

☐ Is confined space entry required?

☐ If yes, are all safety measures being followed?

JOB INFO		
Project/Job	Date	
Contract #	Day	
Location	Weather	
Foreman	AM	PM
Was work delayed for any reason?	☐ Yes ☐ No	Describe in Notes

EMPLOYEES

Employee/General	Hrs	Work Performed

SUBCONTRACTORS

Subcontractor	Men	Hrs	Work Performed

NOTES

ADDITIONAL INFO

Inspections	
Visitors	
Material Delivery	
Equipment on Site	
Rental Tools	

SAFETY

☐ No Injuries	☐ Are there any lifts on the project?
☐ Are project wide power cords in good working condition?	☐ Is the lift's certificate current?
☐ Is project wide fall protection in place?	☐ Are all workers wearing proper PPE?
☐ Are there ladders on the project?	☐ Is confined space entry required?
☐ If yes, have any ladders been modified?	☐ If yes, are all safety measures being followed?

JOB INFO				
Project/Job		Date		
Contract #		Day		
Location		Weather		
Foreman		AM		PM
Was work delayed for any reason?		☐ Yes	☐ No	Describe in Notes

EMPLOYEES

Employee/General	Hrs	Work Performed

SUBCONTRACTORS

Subcontractor	Men	Hrs	Work Performed

NOTES

ADDITIONAL INFO

Inspections	
Visitors	
Material Delivery	
Equipment on Site	
Rental Tools	

SAFETY

☐ No Injuries	☐ Are there any lifts on the project?
☐ Are project wide power cords in good working condition?	☐ Is the lift's certificate current?
☐ Is project wide fall protection in place?	☐ Are all workers wearing proper PPE?
☐ Are there ladders on the project?	☐ Is confined space entry required?
☐ If yes, have any ladders been modified?	☐ If yes, are all safety measures being followed?

JOB INFO			
Project/Job		Date	
Contract #		Day	
Location		Weather	
Foreman		AM	PM
Was work delayed for any reason?		☐Yes ☐No Describe in Notes	

EMPLOYEES

Employee/General	Hrs	Work Performed

SUBCONTRACTORS

Subcontractor	Men	Hrs	Work Performed

NOTES

ADDITIONAL INFO

Inspections	
Visitors	
Material Delivery	
Equipment on Site	
Rental Tools	

SAFETY

☐ No Injuries
☐ Are project wide power cords in good working condition?
☐ Is project wide fall protection in place?
☐ Are there ladders on the project?
☐ If yes, have any ladders been modified?

☐ Are there any lifts on the project?
☐ Is the lift's certificate current?
☐ Are all workers wearing proper PPE?
☐ Is confined space entry required?
☐ If yes, are all safety measures being followed?

JOB INFO				
Project/Job		Date		
Contract #		Day		
Location		Weather		
Foreman		AM		PM
Was work delayed for any reason?		☐ Yes ☐ No		Describe in Notes

EMPLOYEES

Employee/General	Hrs	Work Performed

SUBCONTRACTORS

Subcontractor	Men	Hrs	Work Performed

NOTES

ADDITIONAL INFO

Inspections	
Visitors	
Material Delivery	
Equipment on Site	
Rental Tools	

SAFETY

☐ No Injuries

☐ Are project wide power cords in good working condition?

☐ Is project wide fall protection in place?

☐ Are there ladders on the project?

☐ If yes, have any ladders been modified?

☐ Are there any lifts on the project?

☐ Is the lift's certificate current?

☐ Are all workers wearing proper PPE?

☐ Is confined space entry required?

☐ If yes, are all safety measures being followed?

JOB INFO		
Project/Job		Date
Contract #		Day
Location		Weather
Foreman		AM	PM
Was work delayed for any reason?		☐ Yes ☐ No Describe in Notes

EMPLOYEES		
Employee/General	Hrs	Work Performed

SUBCONTRACTORS			
Subcontractor	Men	Hrs	Work Performed

NOTES

ADDITIONAL INFO	
Inspections	
Visitors	
Material Delivery	
Equipment on Site	
Rental Tools	

SAFETY

☐ No Injuries
☐ Are project wide power cords in good working condition?
☐ Is project wide fall protection in place?
☐ Are there ladders on the project?
☐ If yes, have any ladders been modified?

☐ Are there any lifts on the project?
☐ Is the lift's certificate current?
☐ Are all workers wearing proper PPE?
☐ Is confined space entry required?
☐ If yes, are all safety measures being followed?

JOB INFO		
Project/Job	Date	
Contract #	Day	
Location	Weather	
Foreman	AM	PM
Was work delayed for any reason?	☐Yes ☐No	Describe in Notes

EMPLOYEES		
Employee/General	Hrs	Work Performed

SUBCONTRACTORS			
Subcontractor	Men	Hrs	Work Performed

NOTES

ADDITIONAL INFO	
Inspections	
Visitors	
Material Delivery	
Equipment on Site	
Rental Tools	

SAFETY

☐ No Injuries

☐ Are project wide power cords in good working condition?

☐ Is project wide fall protection in place?

☐ Are there ladders on the project?

☐ If yes, have any ladders been modified?

☐ Are there any lifts on the project?

☐ Is the lift's certificate current?

☐ Are all workers wearing proper PPE?

☐ Is confined space entry required?

☐ If yes, are all safety measures being followed?

JOB INFO			
Project/Job		Date	
Contract #		Day	
Location		Weather	
Foreman		AM	PM
Was work delayed for any reason?		☐ Yes ☐ No Describe in Notes	

EMPLOYEES

Employee/General	Hrs	Work Performed

SUBCONTRACTORS

Subcontractor	Men	Hrs	Work Performed

NOTES

ADDITIONAL INFO

Inspections	
Visitors	
Material Delivery	
Equipment on Site	
Rental Tools	

SAFETY

- ☐ No Injuries
- ☐ Are project wide power cords in good working condition?
- ☐ Is project wide fall protection in place?
- ☐ Are there ladders on the project?
- ☐ If yes, have any ladders been modified?

- ☐ Are there any lifts on the project?
- ☐ Is the lift's certificate current?
- ☐ Are all workers wearing proper PPE?
- ☐ Is confined space entry required?
- ☐ If yes, are all safety measures being followed?

JOB INFO		
Project/Job	Date	
Contract #	Day	
Location	Weather	
Foreman	AM	PM
Was work delayed for any reason?	☐ Yes ☐ No	Describe in Notes

EMPLOYEES

Employee/General	Hrs	Work Performed

SUBCONTRACTORS

Subcontractor	Men	Hrs	Work Performed

NOTES

ADDITIONAL INFO

Inspections	
Visitors	
Material Delivery	
Equipment on Site	
Rental Tools	

SAFETY

☐ No Injuries
☐ Are project wide power cords in good working condition?
☐ Is project wide fall protection in place?
☐ Are there ladders on the project?
☐ If yes, have any ladders been modified?

☐ Are there any lifts on the project?
☐ Is the lift's certificate current?
☐ Are all workers wearing proper PPE?
☐ Is confined space entry required?
☐ If yes, are all safety measures being followed?

JOB INFO		
Project/Job	Date	
Contract #	Day	
Location	Weather	
Foreman	AM	PM
Was work delayed for any reason?	☐ Yes ☐ No	Describe in Notes

EMPLOYEES

Employee/General	Hrs	Work Performed

SUBCONTRACTORS

Subcontractor	Men	Hrs	Work Performed

NOTES

ADDITIONAL INFO

Inspections	
Visitors	
Material Delivery	
Equipment on Site	
Rental Tools	

SAFETY

☐ No Injuries
☐ Are project wide power cords in good working condition?
☐ Is project wide fall protection in place?
☐ Are there ladders on the project?
☐ If yes, have any ladders been modified?

☐ Are there any lifts on the project?
☐ Is the lift's certificate current?
☐ Are all workers wearing proper PPE?
☐ Is confined space entry required?
☐ If yes, are all safety measures being followed?

JOB INFO		
Project/Job	Date	
Contract #	Day	
Location	Weather	
Foreman	AM	PM
Was work delayed for any reason?	☐Yes ☐ No	Describe in Notes

EMPLOYEES	Employee/General	Hrs	Work Performed

SUBCONTRACTORS	Subcontractor	Men	Hrs	Work Performed

NOTES	

ADDITIONAL INFO		
Inspections	
Visitors	
Material Delivery	
Equipment on Site	
Rental Tools	

SAFETY		
☐ No Injuries	☐ Are there any lifts on the project?
☐ Are project wide power cords in good working condition?	☐ Is the lift's certificate current?
☐ Is project wide fall protection in place?	☐ Are all workers wearing proper PPE?
☐ Are there ladders on the project?	☐ Is confined space entry required?
☐ If yes, have any ladders been modified?	☐ If yes, are all safety measures being followed?

JOB INFO		
Project/Job		Date
Contract #		Day
Location		Weather
Foreman		AM	PM
Was work delayed for any reason?		☐ Yes ☐ No Describe in Notes

EMPLOYEES

Employee/General	Hrs	Work Performed

SUBCONTRACTORS

Subcontractor	Men	Hrs	Work Performed

NOTES

ADDITIONAL INFO

Inspections	
Visitors	
Material Delivery	
Equipment on Site	
Rental Tools	

SAFETY

☐ No Injuries
☐ Are project wide power cords in good working condition?
☐ Is project wide fall protection in place?
☐ Are there ladders on the project?
☐ If yes, have any ladders been modified?

☐ Are there any lifts on the project?
☐ Is the lift's certificate current?
☐ Are all workers wearing proper PPE?
☐ Is confined space entry required?
☐ If yes, are all safety measures being followed?

JOB INFO		
Project/Job	Date	
Contract #	Day	
Location	Weather	
Foreman	AM	PM
Was work delayed for any reason?	☐ Yes ☐ No	Describe in Notes

EMPLOYEES

Employee/General	Hrs	Work Performed

SUBCONTRACTORS

Subcontractor	Men	Hrs	Work Performed

NOTES

ADDITIONAL INFO

Inspections	
Visitors	
Material Delivery	
Equipment on Site	
Rental Tools	

SAFETY

☐ No Injuries

☐ Are project wide power cords in good working condition?

☐ Is project wide fall protection in place?

☐ Are there ladders on the project?

☐ If yes, have any ladders been modified?

☐ Are there any lifts on the project?

☐ Is the lift's certificate current?

☐ Are all workers wearing proper PPE?

☐ Is confined space entry required?

☐ If yes, are all safety measures being followed?

<table>
<tr><td rowspan="5">JOB INFO</td><td colspan="2">Project/Job</td><td colspan="2">Date</td></tr>
<tr><td colspan="2">Contract #</td><td colspan="2">Day</td></tr>
<tr><td colspan="2">Location</td><td colspan="2">Weather</td></tr>
<tr><td colspan="2">Foreman</td><td>AM</td><td>PM</td></tr>
<tr><td colspan="2">Was work delayed for any reason?</td><td colspan="2">☐ Yes   ☐ No   Describe in Notes</td></tr>
</table>

EMPLOYEES

Employee/General	Hrs	Work Performed

SUBCONTRACTORS

Subcontractor	Men	Hrs	Work Performed

NOTES

ADDITIONAL INFO

Inspections	
Visitors	
Material Delivery	
Equipment on Site	
Rental Tools	

SAFETY

☐ No Injuries   ☐ Are there any lifts on the project?

☐ Are project wide power cords in good working condition?   ☐ Is the lift's certificate current?

☐ Is project wide fall protection in place?   ☐ Are all workers wearing proper PPE?

☐ Are there ladders on the project?   ☐ Is confined space entry required?

☐ If yes, have any ladders been modified?   ☐ If yes, are all safety measures being followed?

JOB INFO				
Project/Job		Date		
Contract #		Day		
Location		Weather		
Foreman		AM		PM
Was work delayed for any reason?		☐ Yes	☐ No	Describe in Notes

EMPLOYEES

Employee/General	Hrs	Work Performed

SUBCONTRACTORS

Subcontractor	Men	Hrs	Work Performed

NOTES

ADDITIONAL INFO

Inspections	
Visitors	
Material Delivery	
Equipment on Site	
Rental Tools	

SAFETY

☐ No Injuries   ☐ Are there any lifts on the project?

☐ Are project wide power cords in good working condition?   ☐ Is the lift's certificate current?

☐ Is project wide fall protection in place?   ☐ Are all workers wearing proper PPE?

☐ Are there ladders on the project?   ☐ Is confined space entry required?

☐ If yes, have any ladders been modified?   ☐ If yes, are all safety measures being followed?

JOB INFO		
Project/Job	Date	
Contract #	Day	
Location	Weather	
Foreman	AM	PM
Was work delayed for any reason?	☐ Yes ☐ No Describe in Notes	

EMPLOYEES

Employee/General	Hrs	Work Performed

SUBCONTRACTORS

Subcontractor	Men	Hrs	Work Performed

NOTES

ADDITIONAL INFO

Inspections	
Visitors	
Material Delivery	
Equipment on Site	
Rental Tools	

SAFETY

☐ No Injuries

☐ Are project wide power cords in good working condition?

☐ Is project wide fall protection in place?

☐ Are there ladders on the project?

☐ If yes, have any ladders been modified?

☐ Are there any lifts on the project?

☐ Is the lift's certificate current?

☐ Are all workers wearing proper PPE?

☐ Is confined space entry required?

☐ If yes, are all safety measures being followed?

JOB INFO				
Project/Job		Date		
Contract #		Day		
Location		Weather		
Foreman		AM		PM
Was work delayed for any reason?		☐ Yes	☐ No	Describe in Notes

EMPLOYEES

Employee/General	Hrs	Work Performed

SUBCONTRACTORS

Subcontractor	Men	Hrs	Work Performed

NOTES

ADDITIONAL INFO

Inspections	
Visitors	
Material Delivery	
Equipment on Site	
Rental Tools	

SAFETY

☐ No Injuries
☐ Are project wide power cords in good working condition?
☐ Is project wide fall protection in place?
☐ Are there ladders on the project?
☐ If yes, have any ladders been modified?

☐ Are there any lifts on the project?
☐ Is the lift's certificate current?
☐ Are all workers wearing proper PPE?
☐ Is confined space entry required?
☐ If yes, are all safety measures being followed?

JOB INFO						
Project/Job				Date		
Contract #				Day		
Location				Weather		
Foreman				AM		PM
Was work delayed for any reason?				☐ Yes	☐ No	Describe in Notes

EMPLOYEES		
Employee/General	Hrs	Work Performed

SUBCONTRACTORS			
Subcontractor	Men	Hrs	Work Performed

NOTES

ADDITIONAL INFO	
Inspections	
Visitors	
Material Delivery	
Equipment on Site	
Rental Tools	

SAFETY

☐ No Injuries

☐ Are project wide power cords in good working condition?

☐ Is project wide fall protection in place?

☐ Are there ladders on the project?

☐ If yes, have any ladders been modified?

☐ Are there any lifts on the project?

☐ Is the lift's certificate current?

☐ Are all workers wearing proper PPE?

☐ Is confined space entry required?

☐ If yes, are all safety measures being followed?

JOB INFO			
Project/Job		Date	
Contract #		Day	
Location		Weather	
Foreman		AM	PM
Was work delayed for any reason?		☐ Yes ☐ No	Describe in Notes

EMPLOYEES

Employee/General	Hrs	Work Performed

SUBCONTRACTORS

Subcontractor	Men	Hrs	Work Performed

NOTES

ADDITIONAL INFO

Inspections	
Visitors	
Material Delivery	
Equipment on Site	
Rental Tools	

SAFETY

☐ No Injuries
☐ Are project wide power cords in good working condition?
☐ Is project wide fall protection in place?
☐ Are there ladders on the project?
☐ If yes, have any ladders been modified?

☐ Are there any lifts on the project?
☐ Is the lift's certificate current?
☐ Are all workers wearing proper PPE?
☐ Is confined space entry required?
☐ If yes, are all safety measures being followed?

JOB INFO		
Project/Job		Date
Contract #		Day
Location		Weather
Foreman		AM	PM
Was work delayed for any reason?		☐ Yes ☐ No Describe in Notes

EMPLOYEES

Employee/General	Hrs	Work Performed

SUBCONTRACTORS

Subcontractor	Men	Hrs	Work Performed

NOTES

ADDITIONAL INFO

Inspections	
Visitors	
Material Delivery	
Equipment on Site	
Rental Tools	

SAFETY

☐ No Injuries

☐ Are project wide power cords in good working condition?

☐ Is project wide fall protection in place?

☐ Are there ladders on the project?

☐ If yes, have any ladders been modified?

☐ Are there any lifts on the project?

☐ Is the lift's certificate current?

☐ Are all workers wearing proper PPE?

☐ Is confined space entry required?

☐ If yes, are all safety measures being followed?

JOB INFO				
Project/Job		Date		
Contract #		Day		
Location		Weather		
Foreman		AM		PM
Was work delayed for any reason?		☐ Yes	☐ No	Describe in Notes

EMPLOYEES		
Employee/General	Hrs	Work Performed

SUBCONTRACTORS			
Subcontractor	Men	Hrs	Work Performed

NOTES

ADDITIONAL INFO	
Inspections	
Visitors	
Material Delivery	
Equipment on Site	
Rental Tools	

SAFETY

☐ No Injuries   ☐ Are there any lifts on the project?

☐ Are project wide power cords in good working condition?   ☐ Is the lift's certificate current?

☐ Is project wide fall protection in place?   ☐ Are all workers wearing proper PPE?

☐ Are there ladders on the project?   ☐ Is confined space entry required?

☐ If yes, have any ladders been modified?   ☐ If yes, are all safety measures being followed?

JOB INFO			
Project/Job		Date	
Contract #		Day	
Location		Weather	
Foreman		AM	PM
Was work delayed for any reason?		☐ Yes ☐ No Describe in Notes	

EMPLOYEES

Employee/General	Hrs	Work Performed

SUBCONTRACTORS

Subcontractor	Men	Hrs	Work Performed

NOTES

ADDITIONAL INFO

Inspections	
Visitors	
Material Delivery	
Equipment on Site	
Rental Tools	

SAFETY

☐ No Injuries
☐ Are project wide power cords in good working condition?
☐ Is project wide fall protection in place?
☐ Are there ladders on the project?
☐ If yes, have any ladders been modified?

☐ Are there any lifts on the project?
☐ Is the lift's certificate current?
☐ Are all workers wearing proper PPE?
☐ Is confined space entry required?
☐ If yes, are all safety measures being followed?

JOB INFO				
Project/Job		Date		
Contract #		Day		
Location		Weather		
Foreman		AM		PM
Was work delayed for any reason?		☐ Yes	☐ No	Describe in Notes

EMPLOYEES

Employee/General	Hrs	Work Performed

SUBCONTRACTORS

Subcontractor	Men	Hrs	Work Performed

NOTES

ADDITIONAL INFO

Inspections	
Visitors	
Material Delivery	
Equipment on Site	
Rental Tools	

SAFETY

☐ No Injuries
☐ Are project wide power cords in good working condition?
☐ Is project wide fall protection in place?
☐ Are there ladders on the project?
☐ If yes, have any ladders been modified?

☐ Are there any lifts on the project?
☐ Is the lift's certificate current?
☐ Are all workers wearing proper PPE?
☐ Is confined space entry required?
☐ If yes, are all safety measures being followed?

JOB INFO		
Project/Job	Date	
Contract #	Day	
Location	Weather	
Foreman	AM	PM
Was work delayed for any reason?	☐ Yes ☐ No Describe in Notes	

EMPLOYEES

Employee/General	Hrs	Work Performed

SUBCONTRACTORS

Subcontractor	Men	Hrs	Work Performed

NOTES

ADDITIONAL INFO

Inspections	
Visitors	
Material Delivery	
Equipment on Site	
Rental Tools	

SAFETY

☐ No Injuries

☐ Are project wide power cords in good working condition?

☐ Is project wide fall protection in place?

☐ Are there ladders on the project?

☐ If yes, have any ladders been modified?

☐ Are there any lifts on the project?

☐ Is the lift's certificate current?

☐ Are all workers wearing proper PPE?

☐ Is confined space entry required?

☐ If yes, are all safety measures being followed?

JOB INFO				
Project/Job		Date		
Contract #		Day		
Location		Weather		
Foreman		AM		PM
Was work delayed for any reason?		☐ Yes ☐ No Describe in Notes		

EMPLOYEES

Employee/General	Hrs	Work Performed

SUBCONTRACTORS

Subcontractor	Men	Hrs	Work Performed

NOTES

ADDITIONAL INFO

Inspections	
Visitors	
Material Delivery	
Equipment on Site	
Rental Tools	

SAFETY

☐ No Injuries
☐ Are project wide power cords in good working condition?
☐ Is project wide fall protection in place?
☐ Are there ladders on the project?
☐ If yes, have any ladders been modified?

☐ Are there any lifts on the project?
☐ Is the lift's certificate current?
☐ Are all workers wearing proper PPE?
☐ Is confined space entry required?
☐ If yes, are all safety measures being followed?

JOB INFO				
Project/Job		Date		
Contract #		Day		
Location		Weather		
Foreman		AM		PM
Was work delayed for any reason?		☐ Yes	☐ No	Describe in Notes

EMPLOYEES

Employee/General	Hrs	Work Performed

SUBCONTRACTORS

Subcontractor	Men	Hrs	Work Performed

NOTES

ADDITIONAL INFO

Inspections	
Visitors	
Material Delivery	
Equipment on Site	
Rental Tools	

SAFETY

☐ No Injuries

☐ Are project wide power cords in good working condition?

☐ Is project wide fall protection in place?

☐ Are there ladders on the project?

☐ If yes, have any ladders been modified?

☐ Are there any lifts on the project?

☐ Is the lift's certificate current?

☐ Are all workers wearing proper PPE?

☐ Is confined space entry required?

☐ If yes, are all safety measures being followed?

JOB INFO	Project/Job	Date
	Contract #	Day
	Location	Weather
	Foreman	AM	PM
	Was work delayed for any reason?	☐ Yes ☐ No Describe in Notes

EMPLOYEES	Employee/General	Hrs	Work Performed

SUBCONTRACTORS	Subcontractor	Men	Hrs	Work Performed

NOTES	

ADDITIONAL INFO		
	Inspections	
	Visitors	
	Material Delivery	
	Equipment on Site	
	Rental Tools	

SAFETY

☐ No Injuries
☐ Are project wide power cords in good working condition?
☐ Is project wide fall protection in place?
☐ Are there ladders on the project?
☐ If yes, have any ladders been modified?

☐ Are there any lifts on the project?
☐ Is the lift's certificate current?
☐ Are all workers wearing proper PPE?
☐ Is confined space entry required?
☐ If yes, are all safety measures being followed?

JOB INFO				
Project/Job		Date		
Contract #		Day		
Location		Weather		
Foreman		AM		PM
Was work delayed for any reason?		☐ Yes ☐ No Describe in Notes		

EMPLOYEES

Employee/General	Hrs	Work Performed

SUBCONTRACTORS

Subcontractor	Men	Hrs	Work Performed

NOTES

ADDITIONAL INFO

Inspections	
Visitors	
Material Delivery	
Equipment on Site	
Rental Tools	

SAFETY

- ☐ No Injuries
- ☐ Are project wide power cords in good working condition?
- ☐ Is project wide fall protection in place?
- ☐ Are there ladders on the project?
- ☐ If yes, have any ladders been modified?

- ☐ Are there any lifts on the project?
- ☐ Is the lift's certificate current?
- ☐ Are all workers wearing proper PPE?
- ☐ Is confined space entry required?
- ☐ If yes, are all safety measures being followed?

JOB INFO				
Project/Job		Date		
Contract #		Day		
Location		Weather		
Foreman		AM		PM
Was work delayed for any reason?		☐ Yes ☐ No		Describe in Notes

EMPLOYEES			
Employee/General	Hrs	Work Performed	

SUBCONTRACTORS			
Subcontractor	Men	Hrs	Work Performed

NOTES

ADDITIONAL INFO	
Inspections	
Visitors	
Material Delivery	
Equipment on Site	
Rental Tools	

SAFETY

☐ No Injuries
☐ Are project wide power cords in good working condition?
☐ Is project wide fall protection in place?
☐ Are there ladders on the project?
☐ If yes, have any ladders been modified?

☐ Are there any lifts on the project?
☐ Is the lift's certificate current?
☐ Are all workers wearing proper PPE?
☐ Is confined space entry required?
☐ If yes, are all safety measures being followed?

JOB INFO					
Project/Job			Date		
Contract #			Day		
Location			Weather		
Foreman			AM		PM
Was work delayed for any reason?			☐ Yes ☐ No	Describe in Notes	

EMPLOYEES

Employee/General	Hrs	Work Performed

SUBCONTRACTORS

Subcontractor	Men	Hrs	Work Performed

NOTES

ADDITIONAL INFO

Inspections	
Visitors	
Material Delivery	
Equipment on Site	
Rental Tools	

SAFETY

☐ No Injuries
☐ Are project wide power cords in good working condition?
☐ Is project wide fall protection in place?
☐ Are there ladders on the project?
☐ If yes, have any ladders been modified?

☐ Are there any lifts on the project?
☐ Is the lift's certificate current?
☐ Are all workers wearing proper PPE?
☐ Is confined space entry required?
☐ If yes, are all safety measures being followed?

JOB INFO		
Project/Job	Date	
Contract #	Day	
Location	Weather	
Foreman	AM	PM
Was work delayed for any reason?	☐ Yes ☐ No	Describe in Notes

EMPLOYEES

Employee/General	Hrs	Work Performed

SUBCONTRACTORS

Subcontractor	Men	Hrs	Work Performed

NOTES

ADDITIONAL INFO

Inspections	
Visitors	
Material Delivery	
Equipment on Site	
Rental Tools	

SAFETY

☐ No Injuries

☐ Are project wide power cords in good working condition?

☐ Is project wide fall protection in place?

☐ Are there ladders on the project?

☐ If yes, have any ladders been modified?

☐ Are there any lifts on the project?

☐ Is the lift's certificate current?

☐ Are all workers wearing proper PPE?

☐ Is confined space entry required?

☐ If yes, are all safety measures being followed?

JOB INFO		
Project/Job	Date	
Contract #	Day	
Location	Weather	
Foreman	AM	PM
Was work delayed for any reason?	☐Yes ☐No	Describe in Notes

EMPLOYEES

Employee/General	Hrs	Work Performed

SUBCONTRACTORS

Subcontractor	Men	Hrs	Work Performed

NOTES

ADDITIONAL INFO

Inspections	
Visitors	
Material Delivery	
Equipment on Site	
Rental Tools	

SAFETY

☐ No Injuries

☐ Are project wide power cords in good working condition?

☐ Is project wide fall protection in place?

☐ Are there ladders on the project?

☐ If yes, have any ladders been modified?

☐ Are there any lifts on the project?

☐ Is the lift's certificate current?

☐ Are all workers wearing proper PPE?

☐ Is confined space entry required?

☐ If yes, are all safety measures being followed?

JOB INFO			
Project/Job		Date	
Contract #		Day	
Location		Weather	
Foreman		AM	PM
Was work delayed for any reason?		☐ Yes ☐ No	Describe in Notes

EMPLOYEES

Employee/General	Hrs	Work Performed

SUBCONTRACTORS

Subcontractor	Men	Hrs	Work Performed

NOTES

ADDITIONAL INFO

Inspections	
Visitors	
Material Delivery	
Equipment on Site	
Rental Tools	

SAFETY

☐ No Injuries

☐ Are project wide power cords in good working condition?

☐ Is project wide fall protection in place?

☐ Are there ladders on the project?

☐ If yes, have any ladders been modified?

☐ Are there any lifts on the project?

☐ Is the lift's certificate current?

☐ Are all workers wearing proper PPE?

☐ Is confined space entry required?

☐ If yes, are all safety measures being followed?

JOB INFO				
Project/Job		Date		
Contract #		Day		
Location		Weather		
Foreman		AM	PM	
Was work delayed for any reason?		☐ Yes ☐ No	Describe in Notes	

EMPLOYEES		
Employee/General	Hrs	Work Performed

SUBCONTRACTORS			
Subcontractor	Men	Hrs	Work Performed

NOTES

ADDITIONAL INFO	
Inspections	
Visitors	
Material Delivery	
Equipment on Site	
Rental Tools	

SAFETY

☐ No Injuries

☐ Are project wide power cords in good working condition?

☐ Is project wide fall protection in place?

☐ Are there ladders on the project?

☐ If yes, have any ladders been modified?

☐ Are there any lifts on the project?

☐ Is the lift's certificate current?

☐ Are all workers wearing proper PPE?

☐ Is confined space entry required?

☐ If yes, are all safety measures being followed?

JOB INFO		
Project/Job	Date	
Contract #	Day	
Location	Weather	
Foreman	AM	PM
Was work delayed for any reason?	☐Yes ☐ No	Describe in Notes

EMPLOYEES

Employee/General	Hrs	Work Performed

SUBCONTRACTORS

Subcontractor	Men	Hrs	Work Performed

NOTES

ADDITIONAL INFO

Inspections	
Visitors	
Material Delivery	
Equipment on Site	
Rental Tools	

SAFETY

☐ No Injuries   ☐ Are there any lifts on the project?

☐ Are project wide power cords in good working condition?   ☐ Is the lift's certificate current?

☐ Is project wide fall protection in place?   ☐ Are all workers wearing proper PPE?

☐ Are there ladders on the project?   ☐ Is confined space entry required?

☐ If yes, have any ladders been modified?   ☐ If yes, are all safety measures being followed?

JOB INFO				
Project/Job		Date		
Contract #		Day		
Location		Weather		
Foreman		AM		PM
Was work delayed for any reason?		☐Yes	☐ No	Describe in Notes

EMPLOYEES

Employee/General	Hrs	Work Performed

SUBCONTRACTORS

Subcontractor	Men	Hrs	Work Performed

NOTES

ADDITIONAL INFO

Inspections	
Visitors	
Material Delivery	
Equipment on Site	
Rental Tools	

SAFETY

☐ No Injuries   ☐ Are there any lifts on the project?

☐ Are project wide power cords in good working condition?   ☐ Is the lift's certificate current?

☐ Is project wide fall protection in place?   ☐ Are all workers wearing proper PPE?

☐ Are there ladders on the project?   ☐ Is confined space entry required?

☐ If yes, have any ladders been modified?   ☐ If yes, are all safety measures being followed?

JOB INFO		
Project/Job	Date	
Contract #	Day	
Location	Weather	
Foreman	AM	PM
Was work delayed for any reason?	☐ Yes ☐ No	Describe in Notes

EMPLOYEES			
Employee/General	Hrs	Work Performed	

SUBCONTRACTORS			
Subcontractor	Men	Hrs	Work Performed

NOTES

ADDITIONAL INFO	
Inspections	
Visitors	
Material Delivery	
Equipment on Site	
Rental Tools	

SAFETY

☐ No Injuries
☐ Are project wide power cords in good working condition?
☐ Is project wide fall protection in place?
☐ Are there ladders on the project?
☐ If yes, have any ladders been modified?

☐ Are there any lifts on the project?
☐ Is the lift's certificate current?
☐ Are all workers wearing proper PPE?
☐ Is confined space entry required?
☐ If yes, are all safety measures being followed?

JOB INFO		
Project/Job	Date	
Contract #	Day	
Location	Weather	
Foreman	AM	PM
Was work delayed for any reason?	☐Yes ☐ No	Describe in Notes

EMPLOYEES		
Employee/General	Hrs	Work Performed

SUBCONTRACTORS			
Subcontractor	Men	Hrs	Work Performed

NOTES

ADDITIONAL INFO	
Inspections	
Visitors	
Material Delivery	
Equipment on Site	
Rental Tools	

SAFETY

☐ No Injuries

☐ Are project wide power cords in good working condition?

☐ Is project wide fall protection in place?

☐ Are there ladders on the project?

☐ If yes, have any ladders been modified?

☐ Are there any lifts on the project?

☐ Is the lift's certificate current?

☐ Are all workers wearing proper PPE?

☐ Is confined space entry required?

☐ If yes, are all safety measures being followed?

JOB INFO		
Project/Job	Date	
Contract #	Day	
Location	Weather	
Foreman	AM	PM
Was work delayed for any reason?	☐ Yes ☐ No	Describe in Notes

EMPLOYEES

Employee/General	Hrs	Work Performed

SUBCONTRACTORS

Subcontractor	Men	Hrs	Work Performed

NOTES

ADDITIONAL INFO

Inspections	
Visitors	
Material Delivery	
Equipment on Site	
Rental Tools	

SAFETY

☐ No Injuries	☐ Are there any lifts on the project?
☐ Are project wide power cords in good working condition?	☐ Is the lift's certificate current?
☐ Is project wide fall protection in place?	☐ Are all workers wearing proper PPE?
☐ Are there ladders on the project?	☐ Is confined space entry required?
☐ If yes, have any ladders been modified?	☐ If yes, are all safety measures being followed?

JOB INFO

Project/Job		Date	
Contract #		Day	
Location		Weather	
Foreman		AM	PM
Was work delayed for any reason?		☐ Yes ☐ No Describe in Notes	

EMPLOYEES

Employee/General	Hrs	Work Performed

SUBCONTRACTORS

Subcontractor	Men	Hrs	Work Performed

NOTES

ADDITIONAL INFO

Inspections	
Visitors	
Material Delivery	
Equipment on Site	
Rental Tools	

SAFETY

☐ No Injuries

☐ Are project wide power cords in good working condition?

☐ Is project wide fall protection in place?

☐ Are there ladders on the project?

☐ If yes, have any ladders been modified?

☐ Are there any lifts on the project?

☐ Is the lift's certificate current?

☐ Are all workers wearing proper PPE?

☐ Is confined space entry required?

☐ If yes, are all safety measures being followed?

JOB INFO				
Project/Job		Date		
Contract #		Day		
Location		Weather		
Foreman		AM		PM
Was work delayed for any reason?		☐ Yes	☐ No	Describe in Notes

EMPLOYEES

Employee/General	Hrs	Work Performed

SUBCONTRACTORS

Subcontractor	Men	Hrs	Work Performed

NOTES

ADDITIONAL INFO

Inspections	
Visitors	
Material Delivery	
Equipment on Site	
Rental Tools	

SAFETY

☐ No Injuries
☐ Are project wide power cords in good working condition?
☐ Is project wide fall protection in place?
☐ Are there ladders on the project?
☐ If yes, have any ladders been modified?

☐ Are there any lifts on the project?
☐ Is the lift's certificate current?
☐ Are all workers wearing proper PPE?
☐ Is confined space entry required?
☐ If yes, are all safety measures being followed?

JOB INFO		
Project/Job	Date	
Contract #	Day	
Location	Weather	
Foreman	AM	PM
Was work delayed for any reason?	☐ Yes ☐ No	Describe in Notes

EMPLOYEES

Employee/General	Hrs	Work Performed

SUBCONTRACTORS

Subcontractor	Men	Hrs	Work Performed

NOTES

ADDITIONAL INFO

Inspections	
Visitors	
Material Delivery	
Equipment on Site	
Rental Tools	

SAFETY

☐ No Injuries

☐ Are project wide power cords in good working condition?

☐ Is project wide fall protection in place?

☐ Are there ladders on the project?

☐ If yes, have any ladders been modified?

☐ Are there any lifts on the project?

☐ Is the lift's certificate current?

☐ Are all workers wearing proper PPE?

☐ Is confined space entry required?

☐ If yes, are all safety measures being followed?

JOB INFO		
Project/Job	Date	
Contract #	Day	
Location	Weather	
Foreman	AM	PM
Was work delayed for any reason?	☐ Yes ☐ No	Describe in Notes

EMPLOYEES	Employee/General	Hrs	Work Performed

SUBCONTRACTORS	Subcontractor	Men	Hrs	Work Performed

NOTES	

ADDITIONAL INFO	
Inspections	
Visitors	
Material Delivery	
Equipment on Site	
Rental Tools	

SAFETY	
☐ No Injuries	☐ Are there any lifts on the project?
☐ Are project wide power cords in good working condition?	☐ Is the lift's certificate current?
☐ Is project wide fall protection in place?	☐ Are all workers wearing proper PPE?
☐ Are there ladders on the project?	☐ Is confined space entry required?
☐ If yes, have any ladders been modified?	☐ If yes, are all safety measures being followed?

JOB INFO				
Project/Job		Date		
Contract #		Day		
Location		Weather		
Foreman		AM	PM	
Was work delayed for any reason?		☐ Yes ☐ No	Describe in Notes	

EMPLOYEES

Employee/General	Hrs	Work Performed

SUBCONTRACTORS

Subcontractor	Men	Hrs	Work Performed

NOTES

ADDITIONAL INFO

Inspections	
Visitors	
Material Delivery	
Equipment on Site	
Rental Tools	

SAFETY

☐ No Injuries	☐ Are there any lifts on the project?
☐ Are project wide power cords in good working condition?	☐ Is the lift's certificate current?
☐ Is project wide fall protection in place?	☐ Are all workers wearing proper PPE?
☐ Are there ladders on the project?	☐ Is confined space entry required?
☐ If yes, have any ladders been modified?	☐ If yes, are all safety measures being followed?

JOB INFO			
Project/Job		Date	
Contract #		Day	
Location		Weather	
Foreman		AM	PM
Was work delayed for any reason?		☐ Yes ☐ No	Describe in Notes

EMPLOYEES

Employee/General	Hrs	Work Performed

SUBCONTRACTORS

Subcontractor	Men	Hrs	Work Performed

NOTES

ADDITIONAL INFO

Inspections	
Visitors	
Material Delivery	
Equipment on Site	
Rental Tools	

SAFETY

☐ No Injuries ☐ Are there any lifts on the project?
☐ Are project wide power cords in good working condition? ☐ Is the lift's certificate current?
☐ Is project wide fall protection in place? ☐ Are all workers wearing proper PPE?
☐ Are there ladders on the project? ☐ Is confined space entry required?
☐ If yes, have any ladders been modified? ☐ If yes, are all safety measures being followed?

JOB INFO			
Project/Job		Date	
Contract #		Day	
Location		Weather	
Foreman		AM	PM
Was work delayed for any reason?		☐ Yes ☐ No	Describe in Notes

EMPLOYEES		
Employee/General	Hrs	Work Performed

SUBCONTRACTORS			
Subcontractor	Men	Hrs	Work Performed

NOTES

ADDITIONAL INFO	
Inspections	
Visitors	
Material Delivery	
Equipment on Site	
Rental Tools	

SAFETY	
☐ No Injuries	☐ Are there any lifts on the project?
☐ Are project wide power cords in good working condition?	☐ Is the lift's certificate current?
☐ Is project wide fall protection in place?	☐ Are all workers wearing proper PPE?
☐ Are there ladders on the project?	☐ Is confined space entry required?
☐ If yes, have any ladders been modified?	☐ If yes, are all safety measures being followed?

JOB INFO		
Project/Job	Date	
Contract #	Day	
Location	Weather	
Foreman	AM	PM
Was work delayed for any reason?	☐Yes ☐ No	Describe in Notes

EMPLOYEES

Employee/General	Hrs	Work Performed

SUBCONTRACTORS

Subcontractor	Men	Hrs	Work Performed

NOTES

ADDITIONAL INFO

Inspections	
Visitors	
Material Delivery	
Equipment on Site	
Rental Tools	

SAFETY

☐ No Injuries   ☐ Are there any lifts on the project?
☐ Are project wide power cords in good working condition?   ☐ Is the lift's certificate current?
☐ Is project wide fall protection in place?   ☐ Are all workers wearing proper PPE?
☐ Are there ladders on the project?   ☐ Is confined space entry required?
☐ If yes, have any ladders been modified?   ☐ If yes, are all safety measures being followed?

JOB INFO		
Project/Job	Date	
Contract #	Day	
Location	Weather	
Foreman	AM	PM
Was work delayed for any reason?	☐Yes ☐ No Describe in Notes	

EMPLOYEES

Employee/General	Hrs	Work Performed

SUBCONTRACTORS

Subcontractor	Men	Hrs	Work Performed

NOTES

ADDITIONAL INFO

Inspections	
Visitors	
Material Delivery	
Equipment on Site	
Rental Tools	

SAFETY

☐ No Injuries   ☐ Are there any lifts on the project?

☐ Are project wide power cords in good working condition?   ☐ Is the lift's certificate current?

☐ Is project wide fall protection in place?   ☐ Are all workers wearing proper PPE?

☐ Are there ladders on the project?   ☐ Is confined space entry required?

☐ If yes, have any ladders been modified?   ☐ If yes, are all safety measures being followed?

JOB INFO		
Project/Job	Date	
Contract #	Day	
Location	Weather	
Foreman	AM	PM
Was work delayed for any reason?	☐ Yes ☐ No	Describe in Notes

EMPLOYEES

Employee/General	Hrs	Work Performed

SUBCONTRACTORS

Subcontractor	Men	Hrs	Work Performed

NOTES

ADDITIONAL INFO

Inspections	
Visitors	
Material Delivery	
Equipment on Site	
Rental Tools	

SAFETY

☐ No Injuries
☐ Are project wide power cords in good working condition?
☐ Is project wide fall protection in place?
☐ Are there ladders on the project?
☐ If yes, have any ladders been modified?

☐ Are there any lifts on the project?
☐ Is the lift's certificate current?
☐ Are all workers wearing proper PPE?
☐ Is confined space entry required?
☐ If yes, are all safety measures being followed?

JOB INFO				
Project/Job		Date		
Contract #		Day		
Location		Weather		
Foreman		AM		PM
Was work delayed for any reason?		☐ Yes	☐ No	Describe in Notes

EMPLOYEES

Employee/General	Hrs	Work Performed

SUBCONTRACTORS

Subcontractor	Men	Hrs	Work Performed

NOTES

ADDITIONAL INFO

Inspections	
Visitors	
Material Delivery	
Equipment on Site	
Rental Tools	

SAFETY

☐ No Injuries

☐ Are project wide power cords in good working condition?

☐ Is project wide fall protection in place?

☐ Are there ladders on the project?

☐ If yes, have any ladders been modified?

☐ Are there any lifts on the project?

☐ Is the lift's certificate current?

☐ Are all workers wearing proper PPE?

☐ Is confined space entry required?

☐ If yes, are all safety measures being followed?

JOB INFO			
Project/Job		Date	
Contract #		Day	
Location		Weather	
Foreman		AM	PM
Was work delayed for any reason?		☐ Yes ☐ No	Describe in Notes

EMPLOYEES

Employee/General	Hrs	Work Performed

SUBCONTRACTORS

Subcontractor	Men	Hrs	Work Performed

NOTES

ADDITIONAL INFO

Inspections	
Visitors	
Material Delivery	
Equipment on Site	
Rental Tools	

SAFETY

☐ No Injuries	☐ Are there any lifts on the project?
☐ Are project wide power cords in good working condition?	☐ Is the lift's certificate current?
☐ Is project wide fall protection in place?	☐ Are all workers wearing proper PPE?
☐ Are there ladders on the project?	☐ Is confined space entry required?
☐ If yes, have any ladders been modified?	☐ If yes, are all safety measures being followed?

JOB INFO					
	Project/Job		Date		
	Contract #		Day		
	Location		Weather		
	Foreman		AM	PM	
	Was work delayed for any reason?		☐Yes ☐No Describe in Notes		

EMPLOYEES	Employee/General	Hrs	Work Performed

SUBCONTRACTORS	Subcontractor	Men	Hrs	Work Performed

NOTES

ADDITIONAL INFO	
Inspections	
Visitors	
Material Delivery	
Equipment on Site	
Rental Tools	

SAFETY

☐ No Injuries

☐ Are project wide power cords in good working condition?

☐ Is project wide fall protection in place?

☐ Are there ladders on the project?

☐ If yes. have any ladders been modified?

☐ Are there any lifts on the project?

☐ Is the lift's certificate current?

☐ Are all workers wearing proper PPE?

☐ Is confined space entry required?

☐ If yes. are all safety measures being followed?

JOB INFO		
Project/Job	Date	
Contract #	Day	
Location	Weather	
Foreman	AM	PM
Was work delayed for any reason?	☐ Yes ☐ No	Describe in Notes

EMPLOYEES

Employee/General	Hrs	Work Performed

SUBCONTRACTORS

Subcontractor	Men	Hrs	Work Performed

NOTES

ADDITIONAL INFO

Inspections	
Visitors	
Material Delivery	
Equipment on Site	
Rental Tools	

SAFETY

☐ No Injuries
☐ Are project wide power cords in good working condition?
☐ Is project wide fall protection in place?
☐ Are there ladders on the project?
☐ If yes, have any ladders been modified?

☐ Are there any lifts on the project?
☐ Is the lift's certificate current?
☐ Are all workers wearing proper PPE?
☐ Is confined space entry required?
☐ If yes, are all safety measures being followed?

JOB INFO		
Project/Job	Date	
Contract #	Day	
Location	Weather	
Foreman	AM	PM
Was work delayed for any reason?	☐ Yes ☐ No	Describe in Notes

EMPLOYEES	Employee/General	Hrs	Work Performed

SUBCONTRACTORS	Subcontractor	Men	Hrs	Work Performed

NOTES

ADDITIONAL INFO	
Inspections	
Visitors	
Material Delivery	
Equipment on Site	
Rental Tools	

SAFETY

☐ No Injuries
☐ Are project wide power cords in good working condition?
☐ Is project wide fall protection in place?
☐ Are there ladders on the project?
☐ If yes, have any ladders been modified?

☐ Are there any lifts on the project?
☐ Is the lift's certificate current?
☐ Are all workers wearing proper PPE?
☐ Is confined space entry required?
☐ If yes, are all safety measures being followed?

JOB INFO				
Project/Job		Date		
Contract #		Day		
Location		Weather		
Foreman		AM		PM
Was work delayed for any reason?		☐ Yes ☐ No		Describe in Notes

EMPLOYEES			
Employee/General	Hrs	Work Performed	

SUBCONTRACTORS			
Subcontractor	Men	Hrs	Work Performed

NOTES

ADDITIONAL INFO	
Inspections	
Visitors	
Material Delivery	
Equipment on Site	
Rental Tools	

SAFETY

☐ No Injuries

☐ Are project wide power cords in good working condition?

☐ Is project wide fall protection in place?

☐ Are there ladders on the project?

☐ If yes, have any ladders been modified?

☐ Are there any lifts on the project?

☐ Is the lift's certificate current?

☐ Are all workers wearing proper PPE?

☐ Is confined space entry required?

☐ If yes, are all safety measures being followed?

JOB INFO	Project/Job			Date	
	Contract #			Day	
	Location			Weather	
	Foreman			AM	PM
	Was work delayed for any reason?			☐ Yes ☐ No	Describe in Notes

EMPLOYEES	Employee/General	Hrs	Work Performed

SUBCONTRACTORS	Subcontractor	Men	Hrs	Work Performed

NOTES

ADDITIONAL INFO	Inspections	
	Visitors	
	Material Delivery	
	Equipment on Site	
	Rental Tools	

SAFETY

☐ No Injuries
☐ Are project wide power cords in good working condition?
☐ Is project wide fall protection in place?
☐ Are there ladders on the project?
☐ If yes, have any ladders been modified?

☐ Are there any lifts on the project?
☐ Is the lift's certificate current?
☐ Are all workers wearing proper PPE?
☐ Is confined space entry required?
☐ If yes, are all safety measures being followed?

JOB INFO			
Project/Job		Date	
Contract #		Day	
Location		Weather	
Foreman		AM	PM
Was work delayed for any reason?		☐Yes ☐No	Describe in Notes

EMPLOYEES

Employee/General	Hrs	Work Performed

SUBCONTRACTORS

Subcontractor	Men	Hrs	Work Performed

NOTES

ADDITIONAL INFO

Inspections	
Visitors	
Material Delivery	
Equipment on Site	
Rental Tools	

SAFETY

☐ No Injuries
☐ Are project wide power cords in good working condition?
☐ Is project wide fall protection in place?
☐ Are there ladders on the project?
☐ If yes, have any ladders been modified?

☐ Are there any lifts on the project?
☐ Is the lift's certificate current?
☐ Are all workers wearing proper PPE?
☐ Is confined space entry required?
☐ If yes, are all safety measures being followed?

JOB INFO		
Project/Job	Date	
Contract #	Day	
Location	Weather	
Foreman	AM	PM
Was work delayed for any reason?	☐ Yes ☐ No	Describe in Notes

EMPLOYEES

Employee/General	Hrs	Work Performed

SUBCONTRACTORS

Subcontractor	Men	Hrs	Work Performed

NOTES

ADDITIONAL INFO

Inspections	
Visitors	
Material Delivery	
Equipment on Site	
Rental Tools	

SAFETY

☐ No Injuries
☐ Are project wide power cords in good working condition?
☐ Is project wide fall protection in place?
☐ Are there ladders on the project?
☐ If yes, have any ladders been modified?

☐ Are there any lifts on the project?
☐ Is the lift's certificate current?
☐ Are all workers wearing proper PPE?
☐ Is confined space entry required?
☐ If yes, are all safety measures being followed?

JOB INFO		
Project/Job	Date	
Contract #	Day	
Location	Weather	
Foreman	AM	PM
Was work delayed for any reason?	☐ Yes ☐ No	Describe in Notes

EMPLOYEES

Employee/General	Hrs	Work Performed

SUBCONTRACTORS

Subcontractor	Men	Hrs	Work Performed

NOTES

ADDITIONAL INFO

Inspections	
Visitors	
Material Delivery	
Equipment on Site	
Rental Tools	

SAFETY

☐ No Injuries
☐ Are project wide power cords in good working condition?
☐ Is project wide fall protection in place?
☐ Are there ladders on the project?
☐ If yes, have any ladders been modified?

☐ Are there any lifts on the project?
☐ Is the lift's certificate current?
☐ Are all workers wearing proper PPE?
☐ Is confined space entry required?
☐ If yes, are all safety measures being followed?

JOB INFO		
Project/Job	Date	
Contract #	Day	
Location	Weather	
Foreman	AM	PM
Was work delayed for any reason?	☐Yes ☐ No	Describe in Notes

EMPLOYEES

Employee/General	Hrs	Work Performed

SUBCONTRACTORS

Subcontractor	Men	Hrs	Work Performed

NOTES

ADDITIONAL INFO

Inspections	
Visitors	
Material Delivery	
Equipment on Site	
Rental Tools	

SAFETY

☐ No Injuries
☐ Are project wide power cords in good working condition?
☐ Is project wide fall protection in place?
☐ Are there ladders on the project?
☐ If yes, have any ladders been modified?

☐ Are there any lifts on the project?
☐ Is the lift's certificate current?
☐ Are all workers wearing proper PPE?
☐ Is confined space entry required?
☐ If yes, are all safety measures being followed?

JOB INFO				
Project/Job		Date		
Contract #		Day		
Location		Weather		
Foreman		AM		PM
Was work delayed for any reason?		☐ Yes ☐ No Describe in Notes		

EMPLOYEES

Employee/General	Hrs	Work Performed

SUBCONTRACTORS

Subcontractor	Men	Hrs	Work Performed

NOTES

ADDITIONAL INFO

Inspections	
Visitors	
Material Delivery	
Equipment on Site	
Rental Tools	

SAFETY

☐ No Injuries
☐ Are project wide power cords in good working condition?
☐ Is project wide fall protection in place?
☐ Are there ladders on the project?
☐ If yes, have any ladders been modified?

☐ Are there any lifts on the project?
☐ Is the lift's certificate current?
☐ Are all workers wearing proper PPE?
☐ Is confined space entry required?
☐ If yes, are all safety measures being followed?

JOB INFO		
Project/Job	Date	
Contract #	Day	
Location	Weather	
Foreman	AM	PM
Was work delayed for any reason?	☐ Yes ☐ No	Describe in Notes

EMPLOYEES

Employee/General	Hrs	Work Performed

SUBCONTRACTORS

Subcontractor	Men	Hrs	Work Performed

NOTES

ADDITIONAL INFO

Inspections	
Visitors	
Material Delivery	
Equipment on Site	
Rental Tools	

SAFETY

☐ No Injuries
☐ Are project wide power cords in good working condition?
☐ Is project wide fall protection in place?
☐ Are there ladders on the project?
☐ If yes, have any ladders been modified?

☐ Are there any lifts on the project?
☐ Is the lift's certificate current?
☐ Are all workers wearing proper PPE?
☐ Is confined space entry required?
☐ If yes, are all safety measures being followed?

JOB INFO			
Project/Job		Date	
Contract #		Day	
Location		Weather	
Foreman		AM	PM
Was work delayed for any reason?		☐Yes ☐No	Describe in Notes

EMPLOYEES	Employee/General	Hrs	Work Performed

SUBCONTRACTORS	Subcontractor	Men	Hrs	Work Performed

NOTES	

ADDITIONAL INFO		
Inspections	
Visitors	
Material Delivery	
Equipment on Site	
Rental Tools	

SAFETY

☐ No Injuries
☐ Are project wide power cords in good working condition?
☐ Is project wide fall protection in place?
☐ Are there ladders on the project?
☐ If yes, have any ladders been modified?

☐ Are there any lifts on the project?
☐ Is the lift's certificate current?
☐ Are all workers wearing proper PPE?
☐ Is confined space entry required?
☐ If yes, are all safety measures being followed?

JOB INFO		
Project/Job	Date	
Contract #	Day	
Location	Weather	
Foreman	AM	PM
Was work delayed for any reason?	☐ Yes ☐ No	Describe in Notes

EMPLOYEES

Employee/General	Hrs	Work Performed

SUBCONTRACTORS

Subcontractor	Men	Hrs	Work Performed

NOTES

ADDITIONAL INFO

Inspections	
Visitors	
Material Delivery	
Equipment on Site	
Rental Tools	

SAFETY

☐ No Injuries ☐ Are there any lifts on the project?

☐ Are project wide power cords in good working condition? ☐ Is the lift's certificate current?

☐ Is project wide fall protection in place? ☐ Are all workers wearing proper PPE?

☐ Are there ladders on the project? ☐ Is confined space entry required?

☐ If yes, have any ladders been modified? ☐ If yes, are all safety measures being followed?

JOB INFO			
Project/Job		Date	
Contract #		Day	
Location		Weather	
Foreman		AM	PM
Was work delayed for any reason?		☐ Yes ☐ No Describe in Notes	

EMPLOYEES		
Employee/General	Hrs	Work Performed

SUBCONTRACTORS			
Subcontractor	Men	Hrs	Work Performed

NOTES

ADDITIONAL INFO	
Inspections	
Visitors	
Material Delivery	
Equipment on Site	
Rental Tools	

SAFETY

☐ No Injuries
☐ Are project wide power cords in good working condition?
☐ Is project wide fall protection in place?
☐ Are there ladders on the project?
☐ If yes, have any ladders been modified?

☐ Are there any lifts on the project?
☐ Is the lift's certificate current?
☐ Are all workers wearing proper PPE?
☐ Is confined space entry required?
☐ If yes, are all safety measures being followed?

JOB INFO		
Project/Job	Date	
Contract #	Day	
Location	Weather	
Foreman	AM	PM
Was work delayed for any reason?	☐ Yes ☐ No	Describe in Notes

EMPLOYEES

Employee/General	Hrs	Work Performed

SUBCONTRACTORS

Subcontractor	Men	Hrs	Work Performed

NOTES

ADDITIONAL INFO

Inspections	
Visitors	
Material Delivery	
Equipment on Site	
Rental Tools	

SAFETY

☐ No Injuries

☐ Are project wide power cords in good working condition?

☐ Is project wide fall protection in place?

☐ Are there ladders on the project?

☐ If yes, have any ladders been modified?

☐ Are there any lifts on the project?

☐ Is the lift's certificate current?

☐ Are all workers wearing proper PPE?

☐ Is confined space entry required?

☐ If yes, are all safety measures being followed?

JOB INFO			
Project/Job		Date	
Contract #		Day	
Location		Weather	
Foreman		AM	PM
Was work delayed for any reason?		☐ Yes ☐ No	Describe in Notes

EMPLOYEES

Employee/General	Hrs	Work Performed

SUBCONTRACTORS

Subcontractor	Men	Hrs	Work Performed

NOTES

ADDITIONAL INFO

Inspections	
Visitors	
Material Delivery	
Equipment on Site	
Rental Tools	

SAFETY

☐ No Injuries	☐ Are there any lifts on the project?
☐ Are project wide power cords in good working condition?	☐ Is the lift's certificate current?
☐ Is project wide fall protection in place?	☐ Are all workers wearing proper PPE?
☐ Are there ladders on the project?	☐ Is confined space entry required?
☐ If yes, have any ladders been modified?	☐ If yes, are all safety measures being followed?

JOB INFO			
Project/Job		Date	
Contract #		Day	
Location		Weather	
Foreman		AM	PM
Was work delayed for any reason?		☐ Yes ☐ No	Describe in Notes

EMPLOYEES

Employee/General	Hrs	Work Performed

SUBCONTRACTORS

Subcontractor	Men	Hrs	Work Performed

NOTES

ADDITIONAL INFO

Inspections	
Visitors	
Material Delivery	
Equipment on Site	
Rental Tools	

SAFETY

☐ No Injuries	☐ Are there any lifts on the project?
☐ Are project wide power cords in good working condition?	☐ Is the lift's certificate current?
☐ Is project wide fall protection in place?	☐ Are all workers wearing proper PPE?
☐ Are there ladders on the project?	☐ Is confined space entry required?
☐ If yes, have any ladders been modified?	☐ If yes, are all safety measures being followed?

JOB INFO		
Project/Job	Date	
Contract #	Day	
Location	Weather	
Foreman	AM	PM
Was work delayed for any reason?	☐Yes ☐ No	Describe in Notes

EMPLOYEES

Employee/General	Hrs	Work Performed

SUBCONTRACTORS

Subcontractor	Men	Hrs	Work Performed

NOTES

ADDITIONAL INFO

Inspections	
Visitors	
Material Delivery	
Equipment on Site	
Rental Tools	

SAFETY

☐ No Injuries

☐ Are project wide power cords in good working condition?

☐ Is project wide fall protection in place?

☐ Are there ladders on the project?

☐ If yes, have any ladders been modified?

☐ Are there any lifts on the project?

☐ Is the lift's certificate current?

☐ Are all workers wearing proper PPE?

☐ Is confined space entry required?

☐ If yes, are all safety measures being followed?

JOB INFO				
Project/Job		Date		
Contract #		Day		
Location		Weather		
Foreman		AM	PM	
Was work delayed for any reason?		☐ Yes ☐ No	Describe in Notes	

EMPLOYEES

Employee/General	Hrs	Work Performed

SUBCONTRACTORS

Subcontractor	Men	Hrs	Work Performed

NOTES

ADDITIONAL INFO

Inspections	
Visitors	
Material Delivery	
Equipment on Site	
Rental Tools	

SAFETY

☐ No Injuries
☐ Are project wide power cords in good working condition?
☐ Is project wide fall protection in place?
☐ Are there ladders on the project?
☐ If yes, have any ladders been modified?

☐ Are there any lifts on the project?
☐ Is the lift's certificate current?
☐ Are all workers wearing proper PPE?
☐ Is confined space entry required?
☐ If yes, are all safety measures being followed?

JOB INFO		
Project/Job	Date	
Contract #	Day	
Location	Weather	
Foreman	AM	PM
Was work delayed for any reason?	☐ Yes ☐ No	Describe in Notes

EMPLOYEES

Employee/General	Hrs	Work Performed

SUBCONTRACTORS

Subcontractor	Men	Hrs	Work Performed

NOTES

ADDITIONAL INFO

Inspections	
Visitors	
Material Delivery	
Equipment on Site	
Rental Tools	

SAFETY

☐ No Injuries	☐ Are there any lifts on the project?
☐ Are project wide power cords in good working condition?	☐ Is the lift's certificate current?
☐ Is project wide fall protection in place?	☐ Are all workers wearing proper PPE?
☐ Are there ladders on the project?	☐ Is confined space entry required?
☐ If yes, have any ladders been modified?	☐ If yes, are all safety measures being followed?

JOB INFO		
Project/Job	Date	
Contract #	Day	
Location	Weather	
Foreman	AM	PM
Was work delayed for any reason?	☐ Yes ☐ No	Describe in Notes

EMPLOYEES

Employee/General	Hrs	Work Performed

SUBCONTRACTORS

Subcontractor	Men	Hrs	Work Performed

NOTES

ADDITIONAL INFO

Inspections	
Visitors	
Material Delivery	
Equipment on Site	
Rental Tools	

SAFETY

☐ No Injuries
☐ Are project wide power cords in good working condition?
☐ Is project wide fall protection in place?
☐ Are there ladders on the project?
☐ If yes, have any ladders been modified?

☐ Are there any lifts on the project?
☐ Is the lift's certificate current?
☐ Are all workers wearing proper PPE?
☐ Is confined space entry required?
☐ If yes, are all safety measures being followed?

JOB INFO		
Project/Job	Date	
Contract #	Day	
Location	Weather	
Foreman	AM	PM
Was work delayed for any reason?	☐Yes ☐ No	Describe in Notes

EMPLOYEES

Employee/General	Hrs	Work Performed

SUBCONTRACTORS

Subcontractor	Men	Hrs	Work Performed

NOTES

ADDITIONAL INFO

Inspections	
Visitors	
Material Delivery	
Equipment on Site	
Rental Tools	

SAFETY

☐ No Injuries   ☐ Are there any lifts on the project?

☐ Are project wide power cords in good working condition?   ☐ Is the lift's certificate current?

☐ Is project wide fall protection in place?   ☐ Are all workers wearing proper PPE?

☐ Are there ladders on the project?   ☐ Is confined space entry required?

☐ If yes, have any ladders been modified?   ☐ If yes, are all safety measures being followed?

JOB INFO			
Project/Job		Date	
Contract #		Day	
Location		Weather	
Foreman		AM	PM
Was work delayed for any reason?		☐ Yes ☐ No Describe in Notes	

EMPLOYEES

Employee/General	Hrs	Work Performed

SUBCONTRACTORS

Subcontractor	Men	Hrs	Work Performed

NOTES

ADDITIONAL INFO

Inspections	
Visitors	
Material Delivery	
Equipment on Site	
Rental Tools	

SAFETY

☐ No Injuries
☐ Are project wide power cords in good working condition?
☐ Is project wide fall protection in place?
☐ Are there ladders on the project?
☐ If yes, have any ladders been modified?

☐ Are there any lifts on the project?
☐ Is the lift's certificate current?
☐ Are all workers wearing proper PPE?
☐ Is confined space entry required?
☐ If yes, are all safety measures being followed?

JOB INFO				
Project/Job		Date		
Contract #		Day		
Location		Weather		
Foreman		AM		PM
Was work delayed for any reason?		☐ Yes	☐ No	Describe in Notes

EMPLOYEES		
Employee/General	Hrs	Work Performed

SUBCONTRACTORS			
Subcontractor	Men	Hrs	Work Performed

NOTES

ADDITIONAL INFO	
Inspections	
Visitors	
Material Delivery	
Equipment on Site	
Rental Tools	

SAFETY

☐ No Injuries
☐ Are project wide power cords in good working condition?
☐ Is project wide fall protection in place?
☐ Are there ladders on the project?
☐ If yes, have any ladders been modified?

☐ Are there any lifts on the project?
☐ Is the lift's certificate current?
☐ Are all workers wearing proper PPE?
☐ Is confined space entry required?
☐ If yes, are all safety measures being followed?

JOB INFO		
Project/Job	Date	
Contract #	Day	
Location	Weather	
Foreman	AM	PM
Was work delayed for any reason?	☐ Yes ☐ No	Describe in Notes

EMPLOYEES		
Employee/General	Hrs	Work Performed

SUBCONTRACTORS			
Subcontractor	Men	Hrs	Work Performed

NOTES

ADDITIONAL INFO	
Inspections	
Visitors	
Material Delivery	
Equipment on Site	
Rental Tools	

SAFETY

☐ No Injuries

☐ Are project wide power cords in good working condition?

☐ Is project wide fall protection in place?

☐ Are there ladders on the project?

☐ If yes, have any ladders been modified?

☐ Are there any lifts on the project?

☐ Is the lift's certificate current?

☐ Are all workers wearing proper PPE?

☐ Is confined space entry required?

☐ If yes, are all safety measures being followed?

JOB INFO		
Project/Job	Date	
Contract #	Day	
Location	Weather	
Foreman	AM	PM
Was work delayed for any reason?	☐Yes ☐No	Describe in Notes

EMPLOYEES

Employee/General	Hrs	Work Performed

SUBCONTRACTORS

Subcontractor	Men	Hrs	Work Performed

NOTES

ADDITIONAL INFO

Inspections	
Visitors	
Material Delivery	
Equipment on Site	
Rental Tools	

SAFETY

☐ No Injuries   ☐ Are there any lifts on the project?

☐ Are project wide power cords in good working condition?   ☐ Is the lift's certificate current?

☐ Is project wide fall protection in place?   ☐ Are all workers wearing proper PPE?

☐ Are there ladders on the project?   ☐ Is confined space entry required?

☐ If yes, have any ladders been modified?   ☐ If yes, are all safety measures being followed?

JOB INFO	Project/Job		Date
	Contract #		Day
	Location		Weather
	Foreman		AM PM
	Was work delayed for any reason?		☐ Yes ☐ No Describe in Notes

EMPLOYEES	Employee/General	Hrs	Work Performed

SUBCONTRACTORS	Subcontractor	Men	Hrs	Work Performed

NOTES	

ADDITIONAL INFO	Inspections	
	Visitors	
	Material Delivery	
	Equipment on Site	
	Rental Tools	

SAFETY

☐ No Injuries
☐ Are project wide power cords in good working condition?
☐ Is project wide fall protection in place?
☐ Are there ladders on the project?
☐ If yes, have any ladders been modified?

☐ Are there any lifts on the project?
☐ Is the lift's certificate current?
☐ Are all workers wearing proper PPE?
☐ Is confined space entry required?
☐ If yes, are all safety measures being followed?

JOB INFO				
Project/Job		Date		
Contract #		Day		
Location		Weather		
Foreman		AM		PM
Was work delayed for any reason?		☐ Yes	☐ No	Describe in Notes

EMPLOYEES			
Employee/General	Hrs	Work Performed	

SUBCONTRACTORS			
Subcontractor	Men	Hrs	Work Performed

NOTES

ADDITIONAL INFO	
Inspections	
Visitors	
Material Delivery	
Equipment on Site	
Rental Tools	

SAFETY

☐ No Injuries   ☐ Are there any lifts on the project?

☐ Are project wide power cords in good working condition?   ☐ Is the lift's certificate current?

☐ Is project wide fall protection in place?   ☐ Are all workers wearing proper PPE?

☐ Are there ladders on the project?   ☐ Is confined space entry required?

☐ If yes, have any ladders been modified?   ☐ If yes, are all safety measures being followed?

JOB INFO					
Project/Job			Date		
Contract #			Day		
Location			Weather		
Foreman			AM		PM
Was work delayed for any reason?			☐ Yes ☐ No Describe in Notes		

EMPLOYEES

Employee/General	Hrs	Work Performed

SUBCONTRACTORS

Subcontractor	Men	Hrs	Work Performed

NOTES

ADDITIONAL INFO

Inspections	
Visitors	
Material Delivery	
Equipment on Site	
Rental Tools	

SAFETY

☐ No Injuries
☐ Are project wide power cords in good working condition?
☐ Is project wide fall protection in place?
☐ Are there ladders on the project?
☐ If yes, have any ladders been modified?

☐ Are there any lifts on the project?
☐ Is the lift's certificate current?
☐ Are all workers wearing proper PPE?
☐ Is confined space entry required?
☐ If yes, are all safety measures being followed?

JOB INFO		
Project/Job	Date	
Contract #	Day	
Location	Weather	
Foreman	AM	PM
Was work delayed for any reason?	☐ Yes ☐ No	Describe in Notes

EMPLOYEES

Employee/General	Hrs	Work Performed

SUBCONTRACTORS

Subcontractor	Men	Hrs	Work Performed

NOTES

ADDITIONAL INFO

Inspections	
Visitors	
Material Delivery	
Equipment on Site	
Rental Tools	

SAFETY

☐ No Injuries
☐ Are project wide power cords in good working condition?
☐ Is project wide fall protection in place?
☐ Are there ladders on the project?
☐ If yes, have any ladders been modified?

☐ Are there any lifts on the project?
☐ Is the lift's certificate current?
☐ Are all workers wearing proper PPE?
☐ Is confined space entry required?
☐ If yes, are all safety measures being followed?

JOB INFO				
Project/Job		Date		
Contract #		Day		
Location		Weather		
Foreman		AM		PM
Was work delayed for any reason?		☐ Yes	☐ No	Describe in Notes

EMPLOYEES

Employee/General	Hrs	Work Performed

SUBCONTRACTORS

Subcontractor	Men	Hrs	Work Performed

NOTES

ADDITIONAL INFO

Inspections	
Visitors	
Material Delivery	
Equipment on Site	
Rental Tools	

SAFETY

☐ No Injuries
☐ Are project wide power cords in good working condition?
☐ Is project wide fall protection in place?
☐ Are there ladders on the project?
☐ If yes, have any ladders been modified?

☐ Are there any lifts on the project?
☐ Is the lift's certificate current?
☐ Are all workers wearing proper PPE?
☐ Is confined space entry required?
☐ If yes, are all safety measures being followed?

Made in the USA
Middletown, DE
10 February 2024

49444290R00071